LEARNING ABOUT LEAVES

Shanna Wrazen

Rosen
REAL
READERS

Rosen Classroom Books and Materials
New York

Leaves grow on trees.

Leaves have many shapes.

Some leaves turn colors in the fall.

Some leaves stay green in
the fall.

Wind blows leaves to the ground in the fall.

New leaves grow in the spring.

WORDS TO KNOW

leaves

shapes

trees